HOW TO GET OUT OF DEBT AND STAY OUT OF DEBT - EASY & PRACTICAL WAYS TO GET OUT OF DEBT FAST

Easy & Practical Ways To Get Out Of Debt Fast

Curtis Siewdass

ABOUT THE AUTHOR

Facilitator

Conducted Financial Seminar

Published Author

How To Make Money - Strategies For Financial Freedom

Author –Quest Magazine

Strategies For Financial Success & Building Wealth Foundations

Featured on   Entrepreneurship Magazine

Speaker   Financial Bank Rally – 3000 Attendees

Group Innovate Ideas

Quick Loans

Utilizing Staff as a Contact Point

        Interviewing Customer Over the Phone

        New Email Procedures

        Referral System

        Eliminating Lines At Branches

        Financial Magazine

        Improving Debt Collection Process

        Improving the Delinquency Process – Credit Balances

        Improving Efficiency

        Improving Loan Drawdown Process

        Improving Teller System

        Reaching The Market

        Converting Branch Into A Sales Team

        Provide discount For Referrals

        Utilizing Delinquency To Increase Sales

        Creating Wealth Plan For Customers

        Creating A Wealth Plan for Staff

        Utilizing Staff Expertise

Conducted Training Session

    Financial Seminar For Staff

        Efficiency & Motivation Seminars For Supervisors

        Staff Growth & Improvement Seminars

Expertise Featured On   CCN TV 6 - Morning Program - 2 Times

CNC3 - Morning Program - 3 Times (Hema Ramkissoon & Askash Samaroo)

WINN TV Ch 12 - Market To Market - 4 Times

IBN - Improving People & Business - 3 Times

IETV Ch 1 - One On One (Vernon Remesar)

Radio Jaagrati - 7 times

Issac 98.1 (Brian Carter) – 4 times

Wrote 3 Articles   Dealing With the CAL Problem (Front Page)

For News Day Business Section   Overview Of The Economy
(Front Page)

How To Explode Profit - Guide For Business Owners (Centerfold)

Facilitator - Seminars   Marketing, Business, Investment, Leadership, Management

Keynote Speaker at   Black Hawks Business Conference

   Pan Caribbean Games

   Republic Bank Ltd Health & Wellness Event

Trincity Tabernacle Business Meeting

   Ingram Business Leaders Conference

   Business Seminar at JITTA

Master Rank - Black Hawk School

Management of Over 200 Senior Staff

(5 Degree Black Belt)

Consultant for Management Team

Business Growth, Investment & Marketing

Senior Manager for 1500 students

Senior Trainer for Advanced Students

Senior Manager   Black Hawk Martial Arts Met with the Following Government Ministers

Former Minister Of Education

I met with the Minister and board of directors. The Main purpose was to streamline the memory methods used by the ministry – thus enabling children to remember syllabus and subsequently be successful at their examinations.

Minister Of Information & Technology

I met with the Minister and advisors and discussed many suggestions for the economy, traffic, renewable energy, farming etc. – An Official Report was forwarded to the Honorable Prime Minister Kamla Persad-Bissessar (as advised by the minister)

Minister in The Ministry Of Works

I spoke with the Minister via the phone and subsequently forwarded numerous suggestions to solve our traffic problems.

Minister of Work & Transport

Met with the minister and his senior planning team providing practical and inexpensive solutions to solve the traffic problems in our country.

Contact Information :- curtis.siewdass@gmail.com

THE SALARY TEST

Meet Frank - He is a hardworking man looking for his soul mate, wants to get married and settle down.

Frank Met a beautiful young woman name Sue ....

They Got Married and had two children…….. Tommy & Sue-Lee

What a wonderful family, unfortunately, there were a few problems….

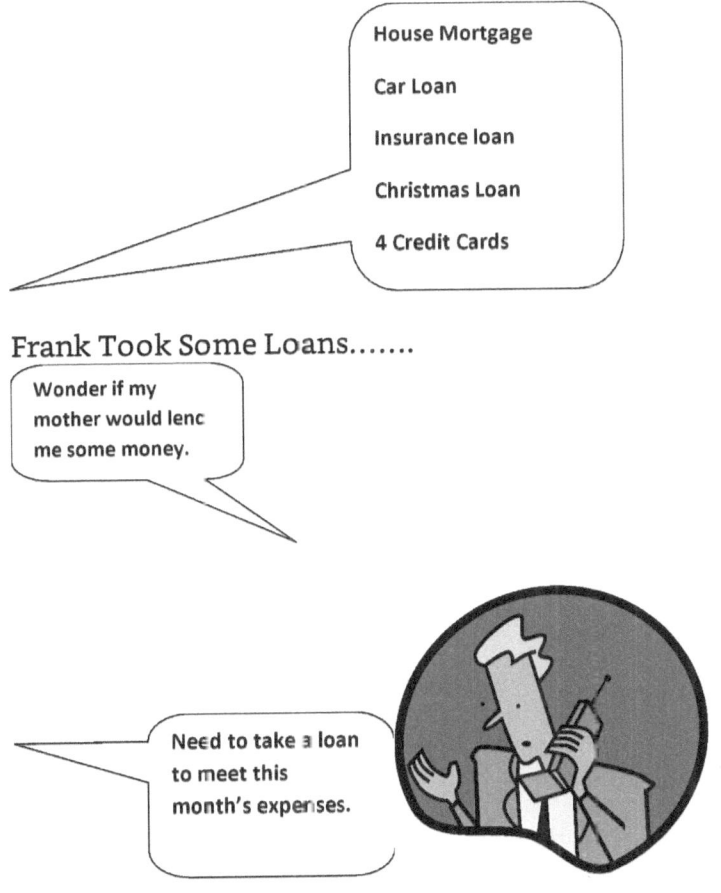

Frank Took Some Loans…….

DEBT IS CAUSED WHEN ONE'S SALARY IS UNABLE TO SUSTAIN MONTHLY PAYMENTS.

LEARN THE SALARY TEST

How Strong is your Salary/Finances?

- Total Loans & Expenses Less Saving = Saving or Loans
- If the answer is loans – divide the figure by your monthly salary

Example
Total Loans & Expenses $50,000.00
Less Savings $10,000.00
Loans $40,000.00
Divide By Salary   ($1,000)   40

It will take 40 months for Frank to clear all his debts….keep in mind this is Frank's full salary and there is no allowance for unexpected expenses.

ALWAYS A SOLUTION

Hey Sue-Lin……

Well it is quite complex and may take some time to master ………..it may take years to understand and many hours of teaching………..just kidding……it is very simple rule…….

Memorise this…..

✓ **For Every Financial Problem , There is <u>always</u> a financial solution!**

Memorise it again…..

✓ **For Every Financial Problem , There is <u>always</u> a financial solution!**

And again…..

✓ **For Every Financial Problem , There is <u>always</u> a financial solution!**

You see Sue-Lin …….debt is only a financial tool used by banks ….as such it is always solvable….

The **memorisation of this rule** will give you hope and the ability to climb up  and find good financial solutions.

Chapter 3

Secura-What?

SECURITY

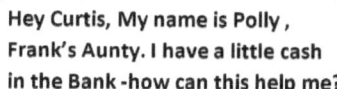
Hey Curtis, My name is Polly, Frank's Aunty. I have a little cash in the Bank -how can this help me?

Hi Polly, I am so glad you asked ...this will help me introduce .....**<u>Understanding Security</u>**

You see banks **love it** if people have money when taking a loan...... it provide some comfort or security for the loan......hence the name security. It simple means, if a loan is fully secured ...there is no loss to the bank.......if partially secured ....there is less loss to the bank ....In most instances the money or security is NOT used, but held by the bank for your loan.....security is also referred to as collateral, however means the same thing.

Security can be ......

- ✓ **A CD or Fixed Deposit Account**
- ✓ **Cash in your Savings or Chequing**
- ✓ **Money Market Fund account**
- ✓ **Shares or Stock in a company** ...some banks are hesitant to accept this because the value fluctuates.
- ✓ **Deed Own Land**
- ✓ **House and Land Together**
- ✓ **Vehicles ....limited depending on the vehicle's age.**
- ✓ **The easier to convert into cash ..the more Banks will accept the security.**

GUARANTOR/SURETY

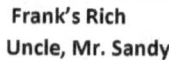 Frank's Rich Uncle, Mr. Sandy

He has lots of Businesses & Money

The Bank Loves Mr. Sandy

He is worth a lot of money, the bank say he has a high net worth.

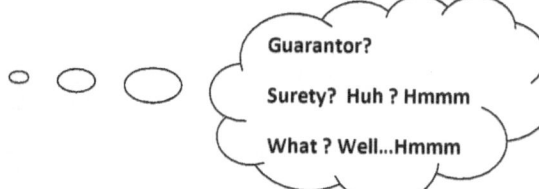

Guarantor?

Surety? Huh? Hmmm

What? Well...Hmmm

Frank Going To Work

Well Frank ...do not look so confused ....actually its much simpler than you think......

A Guarantor or Surety is **anyone** who has money or business value (net worth) and willing to put up his or her money or business value to secure **your loan.** In most instances, a contract to hold their money is required by the bank.

The answer to your next question is ...No...they do not always have to be rich ....the only requirement is to have the monetary ability...

The main reason for guarantors or sureties is to give the bank a better comfort level to grant your loan. If you cannot pay the loan, they have to pay...up to the level they would have signed or agreed.

LOAN AMORTIZATION

I thought you said this was going to be a simple guide .....what gives?

Loan Amortization?.... Huh?

You

Hey, don't start trowing stones yet .....well .... I never......I am going to stop writing this book right now.....yes , I am going to stop writing for one minute.........ok one minute over ....ha ha .... No need to get Angry!

The reason for this big word "amortization" ....is simple.....to help you understand your loan calculation and its benefits.

Loan amortization is simple calculating the length of time allowed by the bank and giving the sum to be paid monthly....it also means interest is calculated on the monthly balance rather than (all interest) at the start of your loan.

It benefits the bank if your balance remains high, but also benefits you if the balance is reduced faster..... in other words - if your loan is amortised or calculated on a smaller balance ...the less interest is paid and the faster the loan is repaid.......

WAIT......Is this allowed by the bank? .....it is recommended you read your loan contract or talk to your bankers to ascertain if there are repercussion......however if you pay your loan on time or quicker.......you are considered a good paying customer and subsequently get good ratings or scores from the bank.

Due to the good credit ratings ....many institutions are more willing to lend money.

GET QUALIFIED

Don't worry, I am not talking about an exam or a test.....simple a means of understanding the loan process…..here is what to do ..... go to your bank and say....

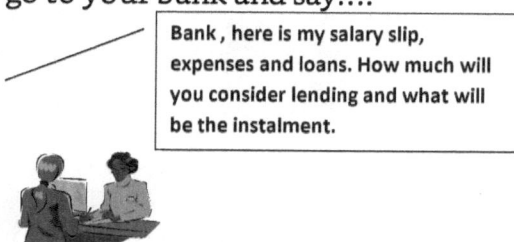

Bank, here is my salary slip, expenses and loans. How much will you consider lending and what will be the instalment.

Before getting rid of your debt, it is important to know exactly how much a financial institution will lend and if you can afford the instalment. The interview will also give an insight into the requirement for the prospective loan.

Most financial institution will calculate 20-40% of your salary as the maximum amount you can afford.

Your Salary

$1,000.

40% $400.

The maximum instalment may not cross $400. – as such getting rid of your debt starts with knowing ...how much money you qualify for.

LOAN BACK-UP PLAN

> Why did I not put a backup plan in place. I have lost my house, car and now my wife is asking for a divorce. Why has this happened...why?

Very soon we will be talking about techniques and strategies to Get Rid of Your Debt, however this chapter is **very important** and must **mastered.** I cannot stress enough the importance of internalising this chapter.

This is what happens to most people....**Loans = No Backup Plan**

If salary stops, this is how it looks....**No Backup Plan = Loss of House, Car etc**

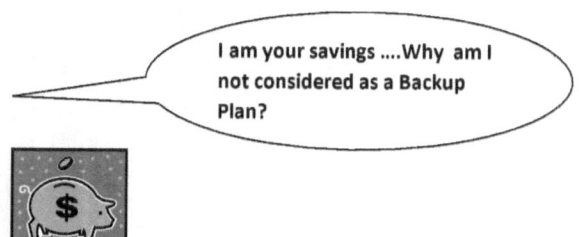

> I am your savings ....Why am I not considered as a Backup Plan?

Well the answer is quite simple .....your brain sees saving as an expendable item ....as such we behave differently to savings....In most instances, saving are not retained and used for personal expenses.

A Loan Backup plan is a sum of money placed in a completely different account and specifically used for emergency loan payment ....here is how...

Over time (6 month – One year) save 3 x 6 times the instalments needed

Monthly Instalment	$1,000.
Backup Plan	$3,000. to $6,000.

The longer the term of the loan …..the greater the backup plan – 12 months instalment. Do not credit to loan, only hold in a separate account for emergencies. **This prevents stress, loss of belongings and allows times for you to get back on your feet.** The time and stress free environment promotes financial recovery.

Let us go over the basics ….. **A Loan Backup Plan is NOT Savings……**The main reason is due to the emotional attachment we have to savings ….. as such this money is spent more easily.

This is what happens when there is **No Loan Backup Plan…….**

No Salary = Loan Going Into Arrears = Loss of House, Car, Etc

A loan backup plan is needed to prevent stress, loss of assets and property.

Step 1   Calculate Monthly Loan Payments (all loans)

Step 2   Over time save 3-6 times the total monthly instalments required.

Step 3   Place in an account that is separate from savings or personal expenses. (not the loan account)

Step 4   If money is utilised, replace as quickly as possible.

Step 5   Do **NOT** use for any expenses other than emergency loan payments which is due to lack or loss of salary / employment.

Important Rule

If the term of your loan is longer than 5 years....it is necessary to save 12 times the total monthly instalment in the loan back up plan account. *(remember this is done over time)*

LOAN DEPRESSION & EMOTIONS

I lost my job, all my loans are in arrears …..I feel so unhappy and depressed……Will I be jailed?

Your loans being in arrears is **not a crime** and in most countries you will not be jailed. It is best to refer your contract to your bankers or attorney to know your rights.

My loans are in arrears and my debt is increasing. I feel so bad about myself ….this has never happened to me.

Remember that your loans are **not a representation of you**, the key is to keep your eyes on the solutions and not the problem….educate yourself and keep a vision of multiple solutions….one always exists!

> I told them I lost my job and cannot pay but the calls keep coming. Do they want me to steal. It is frustrating enough not to have money to feed my family.

Getting angry with a financial institution or with your self does not help the situation. Remember they are only trying to get back their money. On a daily basis, **keep your cool and maintain focus** on being debt free. This will retrain your mind into achieving financial freedom and stability.

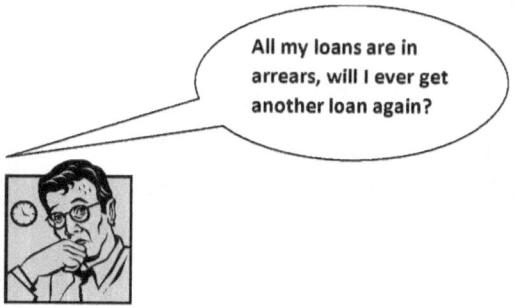

> All my loans are in arrears, will I ever get another loan again?

The direct answer to this question is **Yes**.....while Banks frown upon loans being in arrears ...they also acknowledge improvement in payments ....the thing you must remember ....Banks is in the business of giving loans and once a person meets their criteria......loans are granted....even to those who were once in arrears.

In most democratic countries, financial institutions will **NOT** use any illegal or scary individuals to recovery their money. Reputable companies prefer resolution versus confrontation. The law is very clear and is designed to protect the rights of financial institutions and **You** the individual.

It is unlawful for any financial institution give out financial information to anyone, other than the person who owns the account. The exception to the rule is a high court order.

THE TRUTH ABOUT BANKS

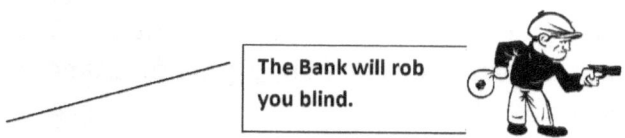

Contrary to rumours and misinformation, Banks are NOT in business to take advantage or rob anyone. Most reputable institution makes an extra effort to ensure exceptional customer service.....even for loan that are in arrears....proper respect and professionalism for You ....the customer is always maintained.

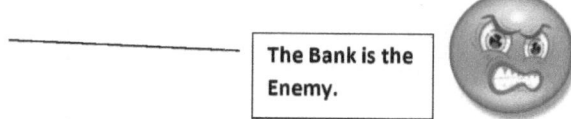

Financial Institutions is not the enemy...Bank make money by giving loans.....this market is so competitive....it will be financial suicide for any institution to be anyone's enemy........Banks provide a valuable service.....assisting anyone who qualifies....to acquire money for personal expenses, vehicle and property. Never view the Bank as an enemy ...view them as a catalyst for your progress.

> They Full their pockets by charging the highest interest rates

The is another misconception held by many individuals.....realistically ....it is in your best interest to shop around for the best rates ....however you have to remember Banks are in the business to make money....they also are keenly aware or their competition.... and often try to offer the lowest rates possible ...to attract the largest number of customers. This means interest rates are often in your favour.

LET'S REVIEW

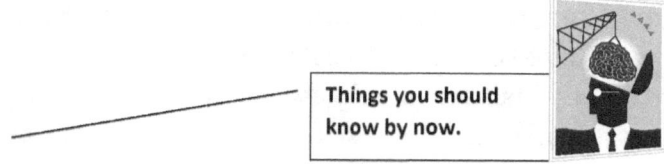

Things you should know by now.

- ✓ What is the Salary Test?
- ✓ Why there is always a solution to Debt?
- ✓ What is security....and why it is important?
- ✓ What is a guarantor or surety?
- ✓ What is the meaning of Loan Amortization?
- ✓ Why Getting qualified is so important?
- ✓ What is a loan back-up plan and ....why is it so important?
- ✓ What is the meaning of loan emotions and depression?
- ✓ Do you know the Truth about Banks?

If any of these questions are giving you trouble please review the previous chapter before progressing .....if you do not understand the basics ...strategy and techniques to get out of debt will be confusing and meaningless.........please take the time

to understand the previous chapters....or else....

THE MOST IMPORTANT RULE
To Learn!

Well...Tell us ...what is the most important rule....come one...out with it ......now please.

RULE ? What Rule .....did I say there was a rule ...feeling woozy..confused...rule ...hmm?

RULE :- If you want to get out of debt , <u>DO NOT</u> repeat to others or make a study of how bad your debt or situation is.

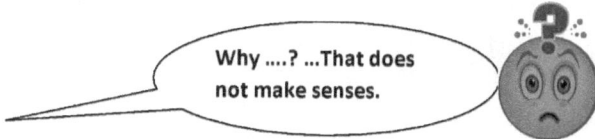

Why ....? ...That does not make senses.

You see....no one can get better if they focus on how bad the situation is ...they get success ....when the brain deliberately focuses on the solutions to the problem.

You will never recover emotionally or financially if you continually fill your mind with images, pictures or ideas of past, present or future doom.

Stop causing your failures to grow stronger , instead repeat everyday the solutions that will be accomplished.

THE UNEMPLOYED

Getting out of Debt when you are unemployed seems very difficult .....in 99% of all cases ......it is the emotional side of being unemployed which prevents progress.

The First Step :- Understand that your situation will never, ever be permanent. Be unemployed is temporary and is **never** permanent.

Second Step :- Understand the art of compounding ……very few people take the time to understand money and compounding …..when they finally internalise the concept …..well…the flood gates fly wide open… you see if I use one hundred dollars ……buy some supplies …..prepare some box lunches and sell each for $25. …..if I sell 10 that day …..i have just made $150. Profit …If this is repeated for 30 days…..i have just made $4,500. ….this is the beauty of compounding …it multiplies you efforts to produce money.

Third Step
Use the part of the money earned to get out of debt. …...

RE-STRUCTURING YOU LOAN

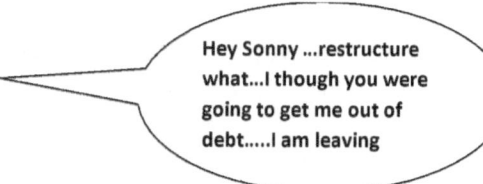

Don't leave yet, mister with the nice hair cut.....restructure is a simple tool that many people are not aware of.....restructuring loan for a longer term and for a smaller instalment (recommended).....the original loan will be repaid and a new one granted for the new terms and conditions.

The answer is Yes.....financial institutions will only restructure if there is a source of income ....however the advantage is you get a smaller instalment ...this means you can now meet personal expense in a better manner ....after a few months –when things have improved ....you can pay extra money to "principal" and repay loan early ...thus paying the same interest.

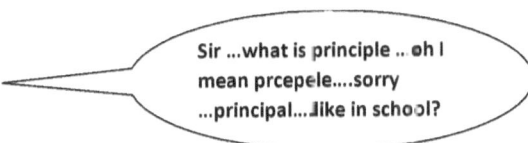

No, it is not referring to a school principal ....how it simple means payment to your loan balance and not to the interest & principal of the loan....this is advantage ....because the smaller the balance to charge interest....the less interest you will have to pay.

Let's go over the procedure
- **Must have a job**
- **Ask financial institution to give a new loan (repaying original)**
- **Ensure that it is for the longest term allowed and smallest instalment.**
- **When thing improve ..pay to principal to repay loan earlier.**

THIS BOOK IS ABOUT SIMPLE, PRACTICAL & EFFECTIVE WAYS TO GET OUT OF DEBT FAST. IT FOCUSES ON CARING FOR THE PERSON AT EVERY LEVEL TO UNDERSTAND SIMPLE CONCEPTS TO MAKE AMAZING CHANGES IN THEIR LIFE!

www.ingramcontent.com/pod-product-compliance
Lightning Source LLC
Chambersburg PA
CBHW031557210526
45464CB00003B/1324